TOMO-CHAN IS A GIRL!

Fumita
Yanagida
Presents

4

Aizawa Tomo

First-year high schooler.
In love with her childhood
friend, Junichiro.
Her family runs a
karate dojo.

Kubota Junichiro

First-year high schooler.
Thinks of Tomo as a friend.
Treats her like a guy.

Gundou Misuzu

First-year high schooler.
Tomo's classmate and best friend.
Childhood friend of Junichiro.
Sharp-tongued.

Carol Olston

First-year high schooler.
British. The school idol.
Kosuke's childhood
friend and fiancée.

Misaki Kosuke

Second-year high
school student.
Men's karate club captain.
The school's prince.

Mifune

Tanabe

Ogawa

CONTENTS

Glad I'm on Her Side

GOOD MORNING, TOMO-CHAN~!

OH. CAROL.

MORNING.

SHE ALWAYS GETS LIKE THIS BEFORE SPORTING EVENTS.

THE DODGEBALL-VOLLEYBALL TOURNAMENT'S COMING UP.

TOMO-CHAN'S SCARY TODAY!

ME TOO.

I'M GLAD WE'RE ON HER TEAM.

5

Don't Stand Behind Me

A Concerning Change

7

Rational Self-Interest

FIGURES.

DODGE-BALL, DUH!

YOU GONNA PLAY DODGE-BALL OR VOLLEY-BALL, TOMO-CHAN?

EVEN IF YOU'RE OUT, I CAN PASS TO YOU IN THE OUTFIELD!

Don't worry about it!

LET'S PLAY TOGETH-ER!

COULD BE LETHAL.

FROM HER...

A PASS...

B-BUT WHY?!

?!

ME TOO!

I'M PLAYING VOLLEY-BALL.

By a Hair

P.E TEACHER, HANAO-SENSEI

EVERYONE'S LIVELY TODAY!

OH MY!

AHH!
EEK!
KYAA!
AHH!

KA—DON

・・・・・・

Shuuu....

SHE MIGHT BE A LITTLE TOO LIVELY.

NO...

Tmp
Tmp

SORRY, TEACH! Y'ALL RIGHT?!

Did it hit you?!

Caution: Hot

TOMO AIZAWA, OF COURSE!

WH-WHO, EXACTLY?

PLEASE!

HANAO-CHAN! DO SOMETHING ABOUT HER!

ISN'T THAT AN EXAGGERATION?

NOW...

DO SOMETHING BEFORE SOMEONE GETS KILLED!

Shake

Shake

THREE?

?

BUT SHE'S... ALREADY POPPED THREE...

RIGHT. I'LL TALK TO HER.

I SEE.

THREE BALLS!

Get Thee Behind Me

WHAT SHOULD I DO ABOUT AIZAWA-SAN?

MAYBE I SHOULD ASK HER FRIENDS TO TALK TO HER.

AS HER TEACHER, I CAN'T TELL HER NOT TO TRY HER HARDEST.

Hmm...

MAYBE I CAN HELP.

REALLY?!

PAT

GUN-DOU-SAN?!

HUH?

DON'T KNOW WHAT TO DO ABOUT TOMO, EH?

I DON'T THINK I CAN KEEP TAKING THE CLASS.

O-OKAY...

I'M REALLY NOT GOOD AT P.E.

BY THE WAY...

ZUuuu...

BLACK-MAIL?!

What a little snake!

CAN YOU HELP ME OUT?

ZUUuuu...

12

Staring into the Abyss

THIS GIRL IS ALSO AIZAWA'S FRIEND.

THAT'S WHY I CALLED HER, BUT...

・・・・・・・

SHE'S KIND OF...

HEL- LOOOO?

MISS?

・・・・・・・

STARING CON- TEST?

IS THIS A...

・・・・・・・

DID I WIN?

SIIIGH ...

GLOOM

I HAVE TO TALK TO AIZAWA MYSELF.

The Bearer of Bad News

I JUST HAVE TO SAY IT...

WELL...

CRACKLE

WHAT'D YOU WANNA TALK ABOUT?!

UM, YES...

YOU CAN TELL?!

HEE HEE!

YOU SURE ARE PUTTING A LOT INTO PRACTICE!

THIS IS THE ONLY TIME I CAN HELP MY CLASS OUT!

I'VE ALWAYS BEEN BAD AT ANY CLASS EXCEPT P.E.

BEFORE SHE BREAKS SOMEONE?

HOW DO I BREAK IT TO HER...

STAB

SO I'M HAPPY TO PUT THE EXTRA WORK IN!

Heh heh!

14

No Reason to Scold Her

HUH?

YES, I DO.

YOU DON'T HAVE TO PUT IN SO MUCH... ENERGY...

A-AIZAWA-SAN, YOU'RE INCREDIBLY STRONG!

IT'D BE DISRESPECTFUL TO THE OPPONENTS AND THE TEACHER!

THERE'S NO MEANING IF I DON'T GIVE EVERYTHING I HAVE!

SHAKE

SHAKE

I SHOULDN'T BE THINKING THIS, BUT...

HUH?! ARE YOU CRYING?!

HA HA HA! OF COURSE...

SHE'S SUCH A GOOD GIRL...

ARGH! SHE'S SO NICE!

I'M HAPPY TO LISTEN.

WHAT'S WRONG, TEACH?

UGHH!

THIS'D BE EASIER IF SHE WEREN'T SO NICE!!

Every Dang Time

WHY'RE YOU BOW-ING?!

Teach?!

HUH?!

I'M SORRY, AIZAWA-SAN!!

BUT...LOTS OF GIRLS WHO **AREN'T** ATHLETIC MIGHT GET HURT BY ONE OF YOUR THROWS...

I WANT YOU TO ENJOY THE TOURNA-MENT...

SO... AIZAWA-SAN...

P-PLEASE GET UP...

AS YOUR TEACHER, I CANNOT PERMIT THAT!

THIS AGAIN?!

WHAT?!

I'D LIKE YOU TO JOIN THE BOYS' TEAM!!

Demons X 2

BE JOINING THE BOYS' DODGEBALL TEAM FOR THE TOURNEY.

Ugh...

AIZAWA-SAN WILL...

FOR VARIOUS REASONS...

SO...

WE GET TO PLAY TOGETHER, TOMO!

Achoo!

WE GOT AIZAWA-SAN!!

Hell yeah!

KUBATA'S SO STRONG THEY NEEDED A HANDICAP?

MAYBE.

MUTTER

NOT ENOUGH PEOPLE?

I DUNNO...

MUTTER

WHY'S THERE A GIRL WITH 1-A?

HEY...

MUTTER

THEY KNEW THEY WERE DOOMED.

THE MEMBERS OF THE KARATE CLUB UNDERSTOOD WHY AND KEPT QUIET ABOUT IT.

A Dark God Descends

18

Offensive Line

Refreshed...?

WHEN YOU'RE DOWN, I'M DOWN.

HUH?

?

SHFF

DON'T WORRY. JUST *GO* FOR IT.

AM I THE ONLY ONE HAPPY ABOUT THAT?

IT'S NOT OFTEN WE'RE ON THE SAME TEAM.

GREAT!!

HAPPY.

BUMP

N-NO! I-I'M...

CAN I GO NEAR HER NOW?

AT LEAST *THIS* WEIRD MOOD SEEMS LIKE A CALM ONE.

TEE HEE!

WIGGLE

WIGGLE

I FEEL LIKE I'M READY TO GO AGAIN!!

But Only Tomo's

TOMO-CHAN
IS A GIRL!

We Don't Need No Warm-Up

EASY!

HA HA! NO WAY!

HEY! WE'RE UP AGAINST THE CLASS WITH THE CHICK!

THE DAY OF THE TOURNA-MENT.

GOOD LUCK!

SURE.

YEAH!

LET'S HAVE A GOOD GAME!

JUST BE READY.

くしゃくしゃと...

DON'T NEED IT.

CRICK

WE'RE K.O.'ED!

THE SLACKER THIRD-YEAR TEAM...

23

Thankfully They Only Got Light Injuries

YOU TOO.

GOOD LUCK.

LET'S HAVE A FAIR GAME!

LET'S HAVE SOME FUN.

EH?

We don't have to hold back with you, senpai!

IT'S JUST DODGE-BALL, MAN...

CALM DOWN!

HA HA!

GUYS! GET READY! THIS IS GOING TO BE A BLOOD-BATH!

MISAKI!!!

URGH!

ZUDON

MISAKI-SENPAI AND HIS LAID-BACK TEAM...

WERE CLEANED OUT.

Tomo's Values

THE OTHER TEAM HAS A FREAKIN' GORILLA!

GUYS! THIS IS BAD!

YEP.

FWIP

NEXT UP IS THE FINALS.

EVEN WE MIGHT NOT BE ABLE TO BEAT HIM.

THEY SAY HE'S STRONGEST IN THE SCHOOL.

FWIP

WE KNOW. THIRD-YEAR, JUDO CLUB. GOUMA TAKERU-SENPAI.

FWIP

YOU DON'T HAVE TO FIGHT HIM, DO YOU?!

FIGHT HIM?!

ME TOO. NEVER THOUGHT IT'D BE THIS SOON.

I KNEW I'D HAVE TO FIGHT HIM SOME-DAY...

HE'S A WORTHY OPPONENT.

I DIDN'T REAL-IZE.

SOR-RY...

AT LEAST ONE MATCH, RIGHT?!

FWIP

OF COURSE WE DO! HE'S STRONGEST IN THE SCHOOL!

FWIP

Like Sisters

A TEAM WITH US ON IT COULD NEVER WIN.

YEAH.

YES, WE DID.

WELL, WE LOST THE VOLLEYBALL TOURNAMENT.

WHAT'S SO FUNNY?

HEE HEE!

TOMO'S FINAL MATCH IS ABOUT TO START.

WE'VE SPENT A *LOT* OF TIME TOGETHER LATELY.

YOU KNOW...

MEAN-IE~!

AW~!

STMP STMP

GRAB

....

As Bad As Each Other

Faint Praise

UH-HUH.

PLEASE.

PLEASE COME AT US WITH ALL YOU'VE GOT.

YEAH.

HUH?

YOU'RE AIZAWA TOMO?

NO WAY THEIR "ACE" IS THIS WEAK LITTLE GIRL!

BUT NOW I SEE THAT'S A JOKE.

I HEARD YOU WERE THE KARATE CLUB'S ACE...

MAYBE YOU'VE GOT SOME STRENGTH.

WHAP

WHAP

"WEAK LITTLE GIRL"?!

Did you hear that?!

What a Waste

YEAH?

KUBOTA, RIGHT?

BUT I'M MORE INTERESTED IN **YOU.**

WHEN I WIN, HOW 'BOUT YOU HAVE TO JOIN THE **JUDO CLUB?**

YOU'VE GOT TALENT, BUT YOU'RE IN THE "GO HOME CLUB"?

AND WHEN *I* WIN...

SURE.

THESE TWO ARE CRAZY.

YOU IDIOT!

Don't ask me!

SMACK

WHAT SHOULD I ASK FOR?

29

Tanabe's Crush(ed)

The boys' dodgeball finals will now begin.

MISUZU-CHAN'S CHEERING FOR ME!

I'M GOING TO WIN THIS...

CLENCH

JUST WATCH, MISUZU-CHAN!

ZU-don

FOR YOU--

DUNNO. I WASN'T PAYING ATTENTION.

DID HE JUST SIGNAL TO YOU?

TA-NABE!!!

The Beam in Your Eye

HEH HEH HEH!

TANABE, YOU ALL RIGHT?

THAT WAS A CHEAP SHOT!

HURTING PEOPLE DOESN'T MATTER IF YOU'RE FOLLOWING THE RULES!

Grip

I'M JUST PLAYING THE GAME.

HE'S GOT A MESSED-UP TAKE ON SPORTS!

WHAT A VIOLENT JERK!

BAS-TARD!

TOTALLY.

THEY'RE ONES TO TALK!

Clash of Perspectives

High Drama

Fight to the Death

CRACK

OH?

LIKE I CARE!

I'LL NEVER FORGIVE YOU!

YOU HIT JUN...

Gwo Gwo Gwo Gwo...

Nod

Nod

UH-OH!

YOU SEEM PRETTY PUMPED, KUBO-JUN...

SHE WON'T LOSE!

DON'T WORRY!

IS SHE GONNA BE OKAY?!

NOW IT'S JUST AIZAWA-SAN AND THE GORILLA!

DON

I'M TAKING YOU DOWN WITH THIS BALL!!!

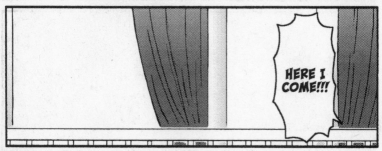

HERE I COME!!!

We're Not Alone

WINNER:
CLASS
I-A

Victory Lap

WHA?!

C'MERE, TOMO!

CON-GRATS!

WAVE

WAVE

Winners of the dodge-ball tournament, class 1-A!

CLAP

CLAP

WHOA!

HEY!

HA HA!

CLAP

Better enjoy it!

Nice one, first years!

Give class 1-A a big round of applause~!

CLAP

CLAP

•••••••

Um, next up...

WHAT?

LEAN~

Nostalgia

YOU SEEM DOWN.

WHAT'S WRONG?

THANKS!

YEAH!

CON-GRATU-LATIONS, TOMO!

IF IT WAS ANYONE BUT JUN, THAT WOULD BE ENOUGH FOR ME.

JUST LIKE OLD TIMES...

I HAD A LOT OF FUN WITH HIM TODAY...

Ha ha!

SORRY, TOMO...

I WISH I COULD DATE HIM BUT STILL DO STUPID STUFF LIKE THIS TOGETHER.

But that's impossible...

I CAN ONLY HELP MYSELF...

BUT IN THE END...

The Thrilla with Gorilla

? HEY, YOU!

TWITCH

TWITCH

'CAUSE I'M NOT!

YOU SATISFIED WITH THAT?

I'M NOT COMPLETELY BURNED OUT.

ALL RIGHT.

WITH-OUT ME?!

JUN DID WHAT?!

SAVAGES.

THAT'S WHAT I HEARD.

Training for War

HOW...?

WHAT... JUST HAP-PENED?

GET THROWN BY SOME KARATE PUNK?!

HOW COULD A JUDO-KA...

AIZAWA-STYLE KARATE ENCOURAGES ITS STUDENTS TO SEE HOW STRONG THEIR BODIES CAN BECOME.

YOU'RE CARE-LESS.

IS HE SERI-OUSLY READY FOR WAR?! But Japan's at peace...

THIS GUY...

YOU CAN'T DEFEAT AN ENEMY WITH JUST STRIKES.

I Get That a Lot

WHEEZE WHEEZE

HAA

HAA

TCH!

SOME- HOW, I WON MORE ROUNDS...

But it was close...

I STILL CAN'T WIN...

YOU'RE A PIECE OF WORK!

?

YOU'RE STILL NOT SATIS- FIED?

YOU FOUGHT IN **MY** STYLE, AND STILL PUT ME THROUGH THE WRINGER...

YOU DIDN'T USE KARATE ONCE.

MAN, YOU'RE ANNOY- ING.

SHEESH.

THAT'S NOT THE PROB- LEM.

The "Why" of Strength

Tomo-zilla

'KAY.

YEAH. I LOST.

SO, YOU HAD A BOUT WITH GOUMA-SENPAI?

YOU KNOW....

I THINK YOU COULD WIN.

I LOST, BUT...

I DON'T THINK SO.

REALLY?

TUMP

YOU GOT ME WAY UP ON SOME PEDESTAL!

I'VE BEEN THINKING...

I'M NOT A DRAGON, MAN.

I WOULDN'T BE SURPRISED IF YOU BREATHED FIRE.

THEN AGAIN...

Still Chasing After Her

I KNOW THAT... I SHOULD KNOW THAT, BUT...

YOUR BODY'S STRONGER. OF COURSE YOU FIGHT BETTER!

YOU'RE A GUY AND I'M A GIRL!

YOU CAME UP WITH THAT ON YOUR OWN.

I DIDN'T THINK ABOUT PASSING THE BALL AT ALL.

I'M WHO I AM BECAUSE OF YOU.

I'M MORE DRIVEN WHEN I'M WITH YOU.

I JUST WANT TO BE LIKE YOU.

OH, NOTHING.

WHAT WRONG? YOU STOPPED.

IT'S NOT ABOUT WHOSE BODY'S STRONGER...

She Said It Out Loud

IT IS!

GOUMA-SENPAI!

OH!

HEY.

YOO-HOO! GORILLA-SENPAI!

SEN-PAI!

YO!

"GORILLA"?

GO-RILLA-SENPAI!

WHAT?

Cute...?

Why? Gorillas are cute!

∧∧ Apologize!!

Act I: They Meet

THE DAY AFTER I MOVED FROM TOKYO...

TEN YEARS AGO...

STARE

I MET HER.

WHA?! HEY! STOP THAT!

?!

clack

H'YUP!

I'M SAYING DON'T CLIMB INTO OTHER PEOPLE'S HOUSES!!

I CAN CLIMB THIS HIGH EASILY!

IT'S NO BIGGIE!

The Boy(?) Next Door

It Snapped Lengthways

HOW'RE YOU SO STRONG?!

ST- STOP! HEY!

YANK YANK

I WANNA PLAY!

DON'T WORRY! I WON'T BREAK IT...

NYA HA HA!

AHHHH! DON'T BREAK IT!

TWO MINUTES LATER.

SNAP...!

ARE YOU A DRAGON?!

WHOOPS, I HELD IT TOO TIGHT.

HOW DID YOU DO THAT?!

Paying with Pain

THWAK

YOU JERK!!!

WH-WHAT HAVE I DONE?!

HE'S BLEEDING...!

AH! I...I PUNCHED HIM.

I JUST BROKE SOMETHING YOU CARED ABOUT...

HUH?

THAT'S NOT ENOUGH.

WHAT'S WITH THIS GUY?!!

I'LL FEEL GUILTY IF YOU DON'T!!

YOU NEED TO PUNCH ME A HUNDRED TIMES!!!

First Impressions

49

A Bear Appears

50

Déjà Vu

UM...

BEGGING IN THE DOORWAY'S A LITTLE...

GLOOM...

TOMO CAUSED YOU A LOT OF TROUBLE.

I COULD NEVER DO THAT...

HE TOLD HIS TERRIFYING DAD?

WAIT...HE WENT HOME AND TOLD HIM WHAT HAPPENED?

Flinch

NO, IT'S FINE...

BUT IS THERE ANYTHING ELSE I CAN DO?

I CAN PAY YOU BACK...

WHOA! LIKE FATHER, LIKE SON!

Rah!

I'LL FEEL GUILTY IF YOU DON'T!!!

ANOTHER ONE?

AKEMI?!

FLINCH

GORO!! WHAT'RE YOU DOING?!

WHY ARE YOU BEHIND ME?

UM...

I'M NOT HARASSING, I'M APOLOGIZING!

DON'T HARASS OUR NEW NEIGHBORS!

NOT AT ALL.

N-NO.

I'M SORRY. LOOKS LIKE MY STUPID FAMILY'S BEING A NUISANCE.

THAT IS A NUISANCE.

OH.

YEAH, THAT WAS MY PLAN.

YOU WERE GOING TO TELL HIM HE CAN TRAIN AT OUR DOJO FOR FREE, RIGHT?

What Was That Feeling?

?

YEAH.

MAKE SURE YOU MAKE UP, TOMO!

I'LL WORK THINGS OUT WITH HIS MOM LATER.

I...I JUST WANT TO BE YOUR FRIEND. IS THAT OKAY?

WE'RE THE SAME AGE, AND NEIGHBORS...

I'M REALLY SORRY I BROKE YOUR GAME.

I FELT SOMETHING WEIRD IN THAT MOMENT.

BA-THUMP

BA-THUMP

UH!

SURE...

REALLY ?!

BUT IT PASSED QUICKLY.

········

YOU SURE YOU DON'T WANNA PUNCH ME?

Right here!

Death Wish

A Glimpse

AND STOP CALLING ME THAT.

DOES IT **LOOK** LIKE I DO?

HEY, GAMER KID! DON'T YOU WANNA PLAY OUTSIDE?

NO! YOU SAY "HEY," "YOU," "MONKEY," AND "IDIOT"!

I DON'T?

HUH?

YOU NEVER CALL ME BY MY NAME.

T-TOMO...

WHOA~!

HUH?

SAY IT AGAIN!

!

FINE... TOMO?

IT WAS A VERY STRESS-FUL TIME.

THIS IS REALLY NOT RIGHT!

THIS ISN'T RIGHT...

I FEEL WEIRDLY HAPPY WHEN YOU SAY IT.

Wonder why~?

BA-THUMP

BA-THUMP

The Measure of Greatness

She's Still Coming

BEAM

UM!

WHAT CAN YOU CATCH HERE?!

BUG HUNTING?!

LET'S GO BUG HUNTING!

← Loves bugs.

THEY'RE DISGUSTING.

I HATE BUGS.

SHE JUST SAID SHE HATES THEM.

LET'S GO!

PAT

LOOKS LIKE MISUZU'S COMING, TOO!

Stairmaster

NO!

DO THEY NOT HAVE THOSE IN TOKYO?

YEAH!

SPARKLE SPARKLE

RHINO-CEROS BEETLES?!

THERE'S A PATH THERE, AND IT'S SUPER CLOSE!

DON'T WORRY!

NYA HA!

ACK!

WE'RE NOT GOING TO HAVE TO CLIMB A CLIFF OR CROSS A RIVER, ARE WE?

LOOKS LIKE TODAY WILL BE LAID-BACK.

REALLY? THAT'S GREAT!

I SHOULD HAVE KNOWN.

THERE'S ONLY 200 OR SO.

IT'S JUST UP THESE STAIRS.

Boys are Stubborn

Lifelong Rivalry Sealed

NYA HA HA! THAT WAS AMAZING!

I'M NUMBER ONE...!

CHECK... IT... OUT...

HAH!

HAH!

HAH!

HUH?

zaa

HOW UN-COUTH.

IS THE *REAL* WINNER.

THE ONE WHO CAN STAND...

AW! THEY'RE FRIENDS ALREADY!

WILL I, NOW?

GWO GWO GWO GWO...

YOU'RE GONNA REGRET THAT!

A Black Gem

IT'S NOT A GIANT ROACH?

Gross...

IT'S A GIANT STAG BEETLE!

Whoa!

WHOA!

CHECK OUT THIS ONE, JUN!

?!

IF YOU BOUGHT THESE IN THE SHOPS THEY'D BE **THOUSANDS OF YEN.**

WOW! I'VE NEVER SEEN A LIVE ONE!

WHAT'S WITH HER?!

LOOKS LIKE MISUZU GETS IT.

HEY!

AMAZ-ING.

61

Fun with Capitalism

NICE ONE!

WOW!

A RHINO BEETLE!

Beam

LOOK, TOMO! I GOT ONE, TOO!

YOU'RE ALWAYS SO POUTY!

HUH? WHAT'S THAT MEAN?

Nya ha ha!

SO, YOU CAN SMILE AFTER ALL!

HMPH! I GUESS... SOMETIMES...

SO? PLAYING OUTSIDE'S NOT SO BAD, RIGHT?

I'M NOTHING LIKE HER.

I'LL SELL THEM TO THE BOYS IN CLASS FOR THIRTY YEN...NO, FIFTY...

HEE HEE...

Store

EVEN MISUZU'S HAVING FUN!

The Start of a Long Battle

The Start of Admiration

YOU RARELY COME OVER HERE, JUN-BOU.

OH?

UM? IS TOMO HOME?

WANNA SEE?

TOMO'S IN KARATE CLASS.

Nya ha ha!

IF TOMO'S BUSY, I'LL GO!

HUH?

THWAM

ONE CHILD IN A CLASS OF ADULTS... SHE NEVER WON, BUT...

HI-YAH!!!

THAT WAS THE FIRST TIME I SAW TOMO SPAR-RING.

SHE WAS SPAR-KLING.

TOMO'S REALLY GOING AT IT!

....

I COULD SEE...

Loves kids.

TOMO-CHAN
IS A GIRL!

No Wild Side Yet

CLIMB-ING A TREE IS **EASY** NOW!

HAH!

YOU'VE REALLY LIVENED UP LATELY!

You don't even cry!

AROUND THREE MONTHS AFTER I MET TOMO...

I WAS MOSTLY USED TO TOMO'S GAMES.

YEAH!

DON'T YOU DARE!

NYA HA HA! I CAN'T CALL YOU A GAMER KID ANY-MORE!

HEY.

I FELT LIKE I WAS GROWING STRON-GER.

HEH!

NICE GAME YOU GOT THERE.

I WAS WRONG.

BUT...

Targets Acquired

HOLD ON! I'M JUST GONNA--

HEY.

HEE HEE!

HEY, I WANNA TRY!

THIS?

WHO'RE YOU?

HUH?

WHERE'D YOU GET THAT GAME?

HE ACTED ALL TOUGH, BUT HE CRIED LIKE A BABY AFTER ONE HIT!

Hilarious!

WE FOUND IT...AFTER SOME NERD DROPPED IT... AFTER WE **PUNCHED** HIM.

YOU CAN SHUT UP NOW.

I SEE.

A Scratch-Covered Smile

No Match for Her

YOU TOOK THEM ON BY YOUR-SELF?!

HUH?

WHAT'S THE BIG IDEA?!

THOSE GUYS ARE AT LEAST THREE YEARS OLDER!

HEY?

WHOA!

CLENCH

HE'S COVERED IN BRUISES!

shove

?!

WHY'D HE DO SOME-THING SO RECK--

MAYBE IT WASN'T THAT RECKLESS!!

URK--

NG...

WHAT THE HECK?!

Frustration

Jun's Vow

I Knew It'd Be Tough

Problematic Role Model

BRING IT ON!

I'M NOT GONNA GO EASY ON YOU.

HOW STRONG YOU GET DEPENDS ON **YOU**.

I'M GOING TO GET STRONGER!

Y-YES, SIR!

WHEN YOU REPLY, YOU SAY, "YES, SIR!"

?!

AKEMI?!

FLINCH

YOU CAN'T JUST TRAIN THIS KID!

HEY! GORO!

JUST LIKE THIS GUY...

JUST LIKE... THIS GUY?

DON'T TALK BACK TO ME!

B-BUT...A PROMISE BETWEEN MEN...

IF YOU LET HIM TRAIN FOR FREE, ALL THE NEIGHBORS WILL WANT TO, TOO!

You ever think about that?!

An Unfulfilled Promise

C'MON! DING

DING

OH! OH!

GAME CLEARED!

CLENCH

DING!

YEAH!!

THAT'S THE UMP-TEENTH TIME NOW.

FLOP

PHEW!

HE'S ALREADY WAY STRONGER THAN ME...

WHEN'S HE GONNA COME GET IT?

TOMO-CHAN
IS A GIRL!

Endangered Angel

I WENT INTO TOWN AND RAN INTO SOMEONE UNEXPECTED.

THOSE GUYS ARE REALLY CROWDING THAT GIRL...

WANNA COME PLAY WITH US? WE'LL KEEP YOU ENTERTAINED!

MOVE, PLEASE.

YOU'RE SO FRICKIN' CUTE! ARE YOU AN ANGEL?

?!

YOU'RE DUMB!

CAROL...

STOP IT!

DUMB AND DUMBER!

SHE SAID IT AGAIN!

YOU'RE DUMB!

WHAT'CHU SAY?! YOU'RE CUTE BUT DON'T--

Role Reversal

Don't Poke the Lion

A Protected Species

Broadening Her Horizons

WHERE ARE YOU TAKING THE TRAIN TO?

HUH?

I DON'T KNOW.

YOU... DON'T KNOW?

WELL...

I'VE NEVER RIDDEN A TRAIN BEFORE.

REALLY?!

REALLY.

MISUZU THOUGHT THAT WAS WEIRD!

"Such a child!"

"Pfft!"

SO I THOUGHT I'D RIDE ONE!

YOU'RE KINDA COMPETITIVE, AREN'T YOU?

83

That's Our Carol

Fluent, But...

I'VE GOT THIS.

E-ENG-LISH?

WHOA!

<EXCUSE ME?>

AMAZ-ING...

WHOA!

JABBER JABBER JABBER

WHAT'D HE ASK YOU?

AREN'T I?!

YOU'RE AMAZING!

THANK YOU!

THE WRONG WAY.

BUT THAT'S...

WHERE THE MUSEUM WAS.

Unfounded Suspicion

GREAT. JUST STAY CLOSE.

WOW! WE'RE AT THE STATION!

WHERE ARE THE TRAINS?

TP TP

HEY! WAIT!!

FIRST, WE NEED TO GET A TICKET...

Flinch

?!

GA-WHACK

I-I DIDN'T DO ANY-THING!!

HUH ?!

STOP THAT.

HEY.

A Fleeting Feeling

YES!

IS IT REALLY THAT FUN?

IT'S LIKE A ROLLER COASTER!

WOW!

CARE...?

IT'S SO FUN, SO WHY DOES NO ONE ELSE SEEM TO CARE?

EVERYONE'S JUST SITTING STILL!

I GUESS WE ALL GROW UP TO BE BORING ADULTS.

THAT'S RIGHT. WHEN I WAS A KID, I WAS EXCITED ABOUT TRAINS...

THAT WAS FAST.

BORED NOW.

THREE MINUTES LATER.

"Heart" Attack?

Evening Girl Talk

Summer Heat

SCREE SCREE

YEAH, IT'S TOO HOT!

Man...

SEEMS LIKE SUMMER'S REALLY KICKED IN.

WANNA GO DURING SUMMER VACATION?

I LOVE THE OCEAN!

OH!

MAKES YOU WANT TO GO TO THE BEACH, HUH?

....

....

OKAY! WHEN?

THEN WE HAVE TO GO AS SOON AS IT STARTS.

YES...

DID YOU HEAR THAT?

Wrong Dress Code

Carol's Standards

ESPE-CIALLY WEARING IT IN FRONT OF THE GUY YOU LIKE.

EVERY-THING.

WHAT'S WRONG WITH THIS?

HUH?

WELL...

RIGHT, CAROL?

IT'S NOT A BIG DEAL...

IT'S THAT BAD?!

SHOCK

I DON'T EVEN WEAR THAT STYLE FOR SWIM CLASS.

YOU HATE IT THAT MUCH?!

IT'S UGLY.

YUP!

A Battleground

COMPLETELY.

YES.

OH, IT'S WRONG.

I DON'T SEE ANYTHING WRONG WITH IT.

Pout

IMAGINE IT.

A BATTLE-GROUND?

THE BEACH IS A BATTLE-GROUND.

LISTEN.

Wanna race to that island?

Yeah!

.....

YOU IN THAT SWIMSUIT WITH JUN-ICHIRO, GOING INTO THE SEA...

NOPE.

I DON'T THINK SHE GETS IT?

I SEE. THIS SUIT **WOULD** MAKE IT HARD TO COMPETE.

Too much water resistance.

Safety in Crowds

NOT THIS AGAIN.

UGH!

LET'S GO SWIMSUIT SHOPPING.

YEAH, I GUESS.

UM...

HUH?

WHICH REMINDS ME, ARE YOU OKAY GOING WITH JUST JUN?

MORE THAN EVER, I THINK...

OF COURSE I DO.

YOU DON'T LIKE HIM ANYMORE?

LATELY... IT'S BEEN JUN WHO'S CHANGED.

SHE HASN'T CHANGED...

WAIT! WHAT ARE YOU MAKING ME SAY?!!

TOMO-CHAN'S SO CUTE! ♡

Acknowledging You Have a Problem

A NORMAL ONE?

SWIM-SUIT?

H-HEY, JUN! WHAT KIND OF SWIMSUIT ARE YOU TAKING TO THE BEACH?

I MEAN WE COULD EVEN TAKE OUR SCHOOL ONES!

RIGHT!

NO. THAT WOULDN'T WORK AT ALL.

WE WERE GOING TO ANYWAY.

PLEASE HELP ME BUY A SWIMSUIT.

Tangled in Curiosity

Faux Pas

IT'S NOT THAT DIFFERENT FROM THE SCHOOL ONE.

I DON'T KNOW.

HEY, MISUZU! HOW 'BOUT THIS ONE?

RIGHT, CAROL ...?

AW C'MON! IT HAS STRIPES! GOOFY **STRIPES**!

Stripes!

UH?

YOUR STRIPES... ARE NICE...

SORRY ...

Double Standard

Data Breach

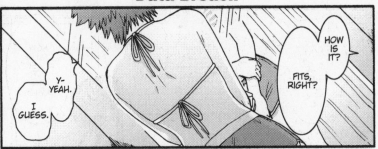

HOW IS IT?

FITS, RIGHT?

Y-YEAH. I GUESS.

HOW?

I'VE BEEN WONDERING...

HOW'D YOU KNOW WHAT SIZE TO GET ME?

You psychic?

EVEN I DON'T KNOW ALL THAT!

WHAT?!

I KNOW YOUR HEIGHT, WEIGHT, BUST, WAIST, AND HIP MEASUREMENTS.

BUT HOW?!

I KNOW THEM, TOO.

The Look

If You'll Have Fun

ABOUT THAT...

YEAH ...

WE STILL GOING TO THE BEACH?

IT'S ALMOST SUMMER VACATION!

COME TOO?

IS IT OKAY IF CAROL AND MISUZU...

THE MORE THE MERRIER, RIGHT?

YEAH ...

HAVE MORE FUN THAT WAY?

WILL YOU...

REALLY ?!

Great!

I THINK SO TOO ...!!

RIGHT. YOU'RE RIGHT...

Grit

TOMO-CHAN
IS A GIRL!

I Blew Up the Innertube

Study in Contrasts

All by Myself!

She'd Do It, Too

HUH?

I HAVE A WHITE BIKINI!

If you outshine Tomo, this is pointless.

Got it?

What kind of swimsuit do you have?

UFK!

I CAN'T BELIEVE YOU'D WEAR THAT IN PUBLIC.

BIKINIS ARE LIKE UNDERWEAR, RIGHT?

THEY'RE THE SAME.

ALL OF IT!

WHAT PART?

BIKINIS AND UNDERWEAR ARE COMPLETELY DIFFERENT.

OKAY, I WAS WRONG.

SHOULD I GO SWIMMING IN MY UNDERWEAR, THEN?

Just Go with It

Zipping into Trouble

Safe Space

L-LET'S GO SWIMMING.

HEY... JUN...

Shff...

THERE'S NO-WHERE ELSE TO SIT.

SHUT UP.

IT'S NOT OFTEN YOU SIT BY ME WILLINGLY.

· · · · · · · ·

WHATEVER DOES **THAT** MEAN?

YOU CAN'T LOOK AT CAROL OR TOMO, BUT YOU CAN SIT NEXT TO **ME**...

Clap

I DIDN'T SAY ANYTHING.

Glare...

I'M GOING TO HIT YOU.

Tomo's New Power

?!

T-TO-MO?!

SOAKED

HEY, JUN! HOW LONG YOU GONNA SIT AROUND?!

SHE'S HAVING SO MUCH FUN SHE FORGOT ABOUT THE BIKINI.

ALL RIGHT! ALL RIGHT!

YANK

GET UP!

TOMO HASN'T EVEN NOTICED...

HEH.

HEY! DON'T PULL ME...!

HURRY UP! THE WAVES ARE FRICKIN' HUGE!

THE ULTIMATE ATTACK.

NYA HA HA!

SHE'S PULLING OFF...

Cups Half Empty

NO WAY?!

AIZAWA TOMO AND BOOBS McGEE ARE HERE.

WHAT?

URK!!

HEE HEE!

HA HA HA!

I DON'T WANNA BE COMPARED TO THAT.

Ah!

SPLASH

Take that!

WHOA. SHE'S SOMETHING WITHOUT A TOP ON.

Damn...

WHO'RE YOU?

I KNOW WHAT YOU MEAN.

Shotgun

A Healthy Man

WHY DOES JUN-KUN KEEP RUNNING FROM TOMO AND ME?

AND WHY'S HE OKAY WITH YOU?

ISN'T IT OBVIOUS?

THESE.

HEE!

POKE

SO, JUN-KUN HATES BOOBS?

NO...

THE OPPOSITE.

HE'S A BOOB MAN.

AND A HUGE PERVERT.

I DON'T GET IT.

Almost There

AND SO LITTLE CLOTHING!

TEE HEE HEE! ♡

SO MANY CUTE GIRLS! ♡

HEY, PART-TIMER! LESS MUMBLING, MORE WORKING!

'KAY.

SIZZ SIZZ

BEACH GUY

I WISH I HAD GIRL-FRIEND.

MAN...

WAIT!!

MISUZU-CHAN?!

Y-YES?

EX-CUSE ME...

DON'T GIVE UP!

You're so close!

ONE YAKISOBA, PLEASE.

YOU'RE... TA... NA...?

Priceless

YOU'RE MY CLASS-MATE.

of course I do.

YOU REMEM-BER?!

I'M JOKING, TANABE-KUN.

?

AND...

AH!

BA-THUMP

YOU'RE... SUCH A NICE GUY...

PAT

THAT REALLY HAP-PENS?!

THEY WERE FREE.

CAN I REALLY HAVE THIS?

How to Split Watermelons

The Beach is Dangerous

TAKE THAT~! HA HA HA HA!

SPLASH

Man!

Whoa~!

BOING

THE BEACH IS **GREAT**, RIGHT, JUN?!

?!

FLINCH

FLINCH

EEK!

GRRRR...

ISN'T IT...?

YOU'RE ON!

OH? A RACE?

LET'S GO IN THE WATER.

Cute? Me?!

?! CUTIE~! HEY, THERE~!

I'M TALKING TO YOU, GIRL!

YEAH!

HUH?

THAT'S NEVER **HAPPENED** BEFORE!

A STRANGE GUY CALLING ME CUTE...?

I GOT A WEIRD ONE...

UM...

WHAT DO YOU **THINK** WHEN YOU SEE ME?! GIVE ME THE DEETS!

The Acoustics Are Better

From Below

Encore

THEN WHY'RE YOU GETTIN' IN MY WAY?!

NO.

HUH?

WHO THE HELL ARE YOU?! HER BOYFRIEND?!

I DON'T LIKE YOU.

FLINCH

EEK!

I DON'T KNOW, BUT...

OFF TOMO.

KEEP YOUR FILTHY HANDS...

SAY IT AGAIN, PLEASE?!

WOOOOW-!

CAN YOU SAY THAT AGAIN?

Say What?!

Double Standard

Proximity

NO, IT'S NOT!!

THAT'S... A RELIEF.

BUT SHE'S FINE?!

YANK

HE SAID IT WAS "BAD" TO BE WITH ME!

WH- WHAT SHOULD I DO?!

REALLY?!

TODAY'S THE PERFECT CHANCE.

WELL, IF YOU WANT TO CHANGE THINGS...

MAKE SURE HE CAN SEE YOU.

GET AT CLOSE TO HIM AS POSSIBLE.

THAT'S ALL.

THAT'S ALL?

....

Meteor

Irresistible

It Means He Likes You

Exhausted

A Critical Moment

NOT REALLY...

HUH?

SOME-THING HAPPEN?

SQUEEZE

DOESN'T LOOK LIKE YOU HAD FUN TODAY.

SOME-THING MIGHT'VE HAPPENED.

WELL...

I STILL DON'T KNOW WHAT'LL COME OF IT...

SMOOCH!

KNEW IT.

TRULY SEES TOMO AS A GIRL NOW.

HEH HEH...

BUT JUNICHI-RO...

Shff...

TOMO-CHAN IS A GIRL!

BONUS CONTENT

Probing Questions

FLEX

Okay~!

SORRY, I'M BUSY THAT DAY.

THE BEACH?

HM?

Oh, that's good. Wish I could go.

Aizawa-san?

TOMO-CHAN'S GOING TOO.

Why wouldn't she? It's the beach...

Huh?

AND SHE'S GONNA WEAR A SWIMSUIT.

Should it?

THAT DOESN'T INTEREST YOU?

No Match

Life Advice

YEAH.

GWO GWO GWO GWO

THERE'S NO HOLDING BACK.

WELL... A MATCH IS A MATCH.

GWO GWO GWO...

WOW...!

THEY'RE NOT THE TYPE TO GO EASY ON ANYONE.

YEAH.

WE NEED TO HOLD OUT FOR AT LEAST **ONE** MATCH.

BECAUSE TRYING TO KEEP UP WITH THEM IN THIS HEAT...

JUST DO WHAT YOU CAN TO STAY OUT OF THE WAY...

GLARE

GLARE

I DON'T WANT TO DIE!

COULD KILL YOU.

Game Start

139

Mountain of Corpses

YOU DON'T NEED TO RUB IT IN.

WE THROTTLED YOU!

DEAD...

NYA HA HA!

WANT ANOTHER ROUND?

LIKE HELL...

OHH? WHAT?

SHUFFLE SHUFFLE

WHAAAA?!!

SHOCK

YANK

I DO!

HEY! COPYCAT!

....

FINE, JUST LET GO!!!

YOU KILLED ME OUT THERE!

This is my revenge!

WHWHAT ARE YOU DOING?!!

TOMO-CHAN IS A GIRL!

Fumita Yanagida

- Now on Twitter @twi_yon
- Volume 5 Coming Soon!

Experience all that SEVEN SEAS has to offer!

Visit us online and follow us on Twitter!
SEVENSEASENTERTAINMENT.COM
TWITTER.COM/GOMANGA

SEVEN SEAS ENTERTAINMENT

TOMO IS A GIRL! Volume 4

story and art by FUMITA YANAGIDA

TRANSLATION
Jennifer O'Donnell

ADAPTATION
T Campbell

LETTERING AND RETOUCH
Carolina Hernández Mendoza

COVER DESIGN
KC Fabellon

PROOFREADER
Danielle King
Stephanie Cohen

EDITOR
Shannon Fay

PRODUCTION MANAGER
Lissa Pattillo

MANAGING EDITOR
Julie Davis

EDITOR-IN-CHIEF
Adam Arnold

PUBLISHER
Jason DeAngelis

TOMO-CHAN WA ONNANOKO! VOL. 4
© Fumita Yanagida 2017
All rights reserved.
First published in Japan in 2017 by Star Seas Company.
Publication rights for this English edition arranged with Star Seas Company
through Kodansha Ltd.,Tokyo.

No portion of this book may be reproduced or transmitted in any form without
written permission from the copyright holders. This is a work of fiction.
Names, characters, places, and incidents are the products of the author's imagination
or are used fictitiously. Any resemblance to actual events, locales, or persons,
living or dead, is entirely coincidental.

Seven Seas press and purchase enquiries can be sent to Marketing Manager
Lianne Sentar at press@gomanga.com. Information regarding the distribution
and purchase of digital editions is available from Digital Manager CK Russell
at digital@gomanga.com.

Seven Seas and the Seven Seas logo are trademarks of
Seven Seas Entertainment. All rights reserved.

ISBN: 978-1-64275-109-3

Printed in Canada

First Printing: July 2019

10 9 8 7 6 5 4 3 2 1

FOLLOW US ONLINE: *www.sevenseasentertainment.com*

READING DIRECTIONS

This book reads from *right to left*, Japanese style.
If this is your first time reading manga, you start
reading from the top right panel on each page and
take it from there. If you get lost, just follow the
numbered diagram here. It may seem backwards at
first, but you'll get the hang of it! Have fun!!

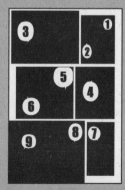